TABLE OF CONTENTS

PHONICS
Initial Consonants	2
Short **a**	3
Short **e**	4
Short **i**	5
Short **o**	6
Short **u**	7
Short Vowel Puzzle	8
Short Vowel Review	9
Long **a**	10
Long **e**	11
Long **i**	12
Long **o**	13
Long **u**	14
Long Vowel Puzzle	15
Long Vowel Review	16

LANGUAGE
Story Order	17
Telling Sentences	18
Asking Sentences	19
Naming Words	20–21
Naming More Than One	22
Action Words	23
Adding 's' to Action Words	24
Describing Words	25–26
Contractions	27

MATH
Addition	28, 30
Subtraction	29, 31
Addition and Subtraction	32, 37–38
Counting On	33
Counting Back	34
Addition Using a Number Line	35
Subtraction Using a Number Line	36
Plane Figures	39
Space Figures	40
Same Size and Shape	41
Counting by Tens	42
Tens and Ones	43–44
Greater Than and Less Than	45
Before, Between and After	46
Counting Coins	47–48
Time: Hours	49
Time: Half Hours	50
Time: Quarter Past the Hour	51
Time: Quarter to the Hour	52
Equal Parts of Wholes	53
Halves, Thirds and Quarters	54
Parts of Groups	55
Picture Graph	56
Adding Three Addends	57
Adding Tens and Ones	58
Subtracting Tens and Ones	59
Addition and Subtraction Review	60

AND MORE...
Answer Key	61–63
Certificate	64

INITIAL CONSONANTS

Write the first letter of each picture's name.
Read the animal names.
Write the problem numbers in the circles by the correct animals.

1. _____

2. _____

3. _____

4. _____

Initial Consonants

SHORT A

Circle the pictures whose names have the **short a** sound.

short a sound
hat

1.

2.

   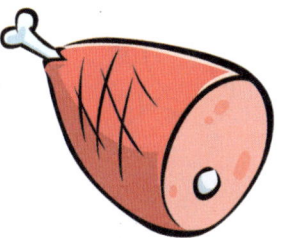

3.

  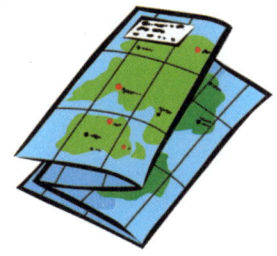 

4.

SHORT E

Circle the pictures whose names have the **short e** sound.

1.

2.

3.

4.

SHORT I

Circle the pictures whose names have the **short i** sound.

short i sound
dish

1.

2.

3.

4.

SHORT O

Circle the pictures whose names have the **short o** sound.

short **o** sound
rock

1.

2.

3.

 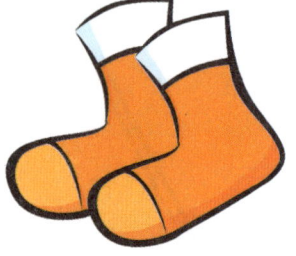  

4.

SHORT U

Circle the pictures whose names have the **short u** sound.

short u sound
drum

1.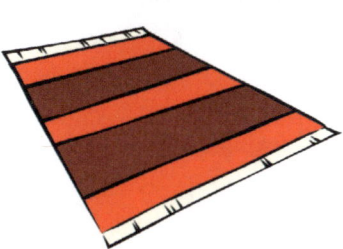

2.

3.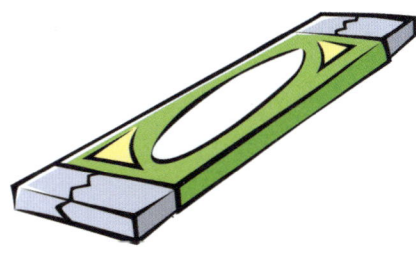

4.

SHORT VOWEL PUZZLE

The letters **a, e, i, o** and **u** are **vowels**.
These words have **short vowel** sounds:

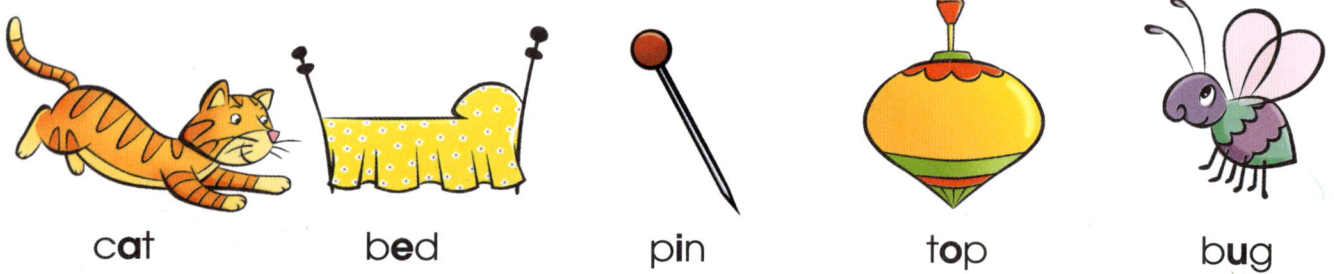

c**a**t   b**e**d   p**i**n   t**o**p   b**u**g

Look at the pictures. Say the words.
Write the short vowels in the puzzle.

ACROSS

2.

3.

5.

DOWN

1.

2.

4.

	1.h		2.s		c	k
	3.t	4.	n			
		g				
	5.p		g			

Short Vowel Puzzle   ©School Zone Publishing Company

SHORT VOWEL REVIEW

Write short vowels to complete the words.

a e i o u
fox

1. t_n 2. c_t 3. p_g

4. b_s 5. d_ll 6. f_n

7. f_sh 8. n_st 9. d_ck

LONG A

Write the **long a** words to answer the riddles.

long a sound
snake

| rain | grate | cake |
| day | gate | snail |

1. I live in a shell.

2. I wear candles on your birthday.

3. I make flowers grow.

4. I am the opposite of night.

5. Write two **long a** words that begin with **g**.

LONG E

Write the **long e** words to answer the riddles.

long e sound
seal

| sheep | leaf | he |
| three | tree | me |

1. I come after two.

2. I grow outside.

3. I say 'baa!'

4. I grow on a tree.

5. Write two two-letter **long e** words.

LONG I

Write the **long i** words to answer the riddles.

long i sound
kite

| ice | right | tie |
| bike | tight | nine |

1. You can ride me.

2. I come before ten.

3. I am very cold.

4. This is the opposite of left.

5. Write two **long i** words that begin with **t**.

LONG O

Write the **long o** words to answer the riddles.

long o sound
coat

rose   goat   rope
nose   boat   note

1. I live on a farm.

2. You can tie things with me.

3. I move in water.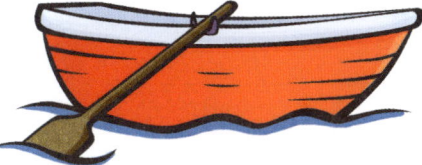

4. I am a kind of flower.

5. Write two **long o** words that begin with **n**.

LONG U

Write the **long u** words to answer the riddles.

long u sound
cube

| cute | tube | new |
| huge | few | glue |

1. Toothpaste comes in a _____.

2. Use me to stick things together. _____

3. A whale is _____.

4. Babies are _____.

5. Write two **long u** words that end with **ew**.
_____   _____

Long u   14   ©School Zone Publishing Company

LONG VOWEL PUZZLE

As you've learned, the letters **a**, **e**, **i**, **o** and **u** are **vowels**.
A **long vowel** says its own name.
These words have **long vowel** sounds:

c**a**ke   tr**ee**   h**i**ve   r**o**pe   m**u**le

Look at the pictures. Say the words.
Write the long vowels in the puzzle.

ACROSS

1.  (rake)
4.  (tube)
6.  (slide)

DOWN

2.  (kite)
3.  (bee)
5.  (bone)

LONG VOWEL REVIEW

Draw lines from the pictures to the long vowel sounds heard in their names.

long a

long e

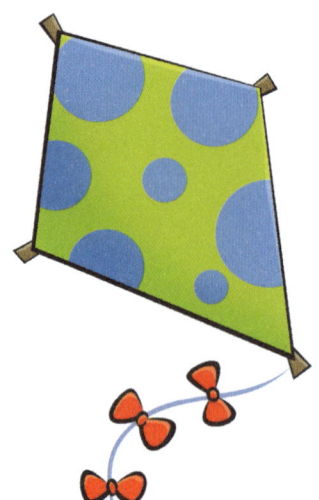

long i

long o

long u

STORY ORDER

Number the pictures from 1 to 6 to show the correct order.

TELLING SENTENCES

A **telling sentence** begins with a capital letter.
It ends with a full stop (.).

Use the ≡ to show where capital letters go.
Then put a full stop (.) at the end of each sentence.
The first one is done for you.

1. <u>o</u>ur dog is hungry.

2. dad brings food

3. skip eats quickly

4. food goes on the floor

5. dogs are messy

6. now I need to clean up

7. Write a telling sentence.

ASKING SENTENCES

An **asking sentence** asks about something or someone.
It ends with a question mark (**?**).

Use the ≡ to show where capital letters go. Then put a question mark (**?**) at the end of each sentence that asks a question and a full stop (**.**) at the end of the telling sentence. The first one is done for you.

1. i̲s̲ Mother home**?**

2. where did she go

3. when will she be back

4. who baked the cookies

5. they are good

6. may I have another one

7. Write an asking sentence.

_____

_____

_____

NAMING WORDS

Some **naming words** name people or animals.

Here are a few examples:
girl   brother   cat   horse

Read the sentences. Write the naming words that name people or animals. The first one is done for you.

1. Dad drove away.

2. The farmer waved. _____

3. The cow was eating. _____

4. Our dog barked. _____

5. A chicken ran away. _____

NAMING WORDS

Some **naming words** name places or things.

Here are a few examples:
    school   **city**   **shoe**   **apple**

Which words name places, and which words name things? Write each word from the box on the correct list.

zoo   house   pizza
book   town   bike

Places

Things

Write a naming word for a place and a naming word for a thing.

Place

Thing

NAMING MORE THAN ONE

Many words add **s** to name **more than one**.

Here are a few examples:
    hens   frogs   rings

Add **s** to the naming words from the box to finish the sentences. The first one is done for you.

| dog   spot   cat |
| bone   ear |

1. Jamie has two  _____ .

2. One dog has brown _____ .

3. One dog has black _____ .

4. They run after _____ .

5. They bury _____ .

ACTION WORDS

An **action word** tells what someone or something does.

Here are a few examples:
     jump   cry   eat   push

Read the sentences. Write the action words.
The first one is done for you.

1. Let's play a game.

2. Jake hits the ball. _____

3. The ball flies high. _____

4. Megan runs after it. _____

5. Will she catch it? _____

ADDING 'S' TO ACTION WORDS

Add **s** to the action words from the box to finish the sentences. The first one is done for you.

| plant | eat | water |
| pull | grow |

1. Each spring, Bob ___**plants**___ a garden.

2. He _____ pretty flowers.

3. Dad _____ weeds.

4. Anna _____ the garden.

5. Sometimes a rabbit _____ the flowers.

DESCRIBING WORDS

Some **describing words** tell how things sound or feel.

Here are a few examples:
   quiet   warm   smooth

| hot | cold | loud |
| wet | | soft |

Write the describing words from the box to finish the sentences. The first one is done for you.

1. The sun is  hot .

2. A jet makes a _____ sound.

3. Ice-cream is _____ .

4. The kitten has _____ fur.

5. Don't slip on the _____ grass.

25

DESCRIBING WORDS

Some **describing words** tell size, colour, number or amount.

Here are a few examples:
small   red   seven

Underline the describing words in the sentences.
The first one is done for you.

1. Lady is a <u>big</u> cat.

2. She has three kittens.

3. Tiger is the striped kitten.

4. Jet is the black kitten.

5. The little kitten is Socks.

6. We now have four cats.

7. Write a sentence using a describing word. Underline the describing word.

CONTRACTIONS

A **contraction** is a short way to write two words.

I am → I'm

haven't   don't   Let's
aren't   won't

Write the contractions for the underlined words. The first one is done for you.

1. Please <u>do not</u> go. _____

2. We <u>are not</u> done. _____

3. We <u>have not</u> painted it. _____

4. <u>Let us</u> paint it red. _____

5. It <u>will not</u> take long. _____

ADDITION

2 + 1 = __3__

3 + 2 = __5__

Add.

1. 3 + 1 = ____

2. 1 + 1 = ____

3. 2 + 2 = ____

4. 1 + 3 = ____

5. 3 + 2 = ____

6. 2 + 1 = ____

SUBTRACTION

4 − 1 = __3__   5 − 2 = __3__

Subtract. Cross out pictures to show the number sentence. Write how many are left.

1. 3 − 1 = ____   2. 4 − 2 = ____

3. 5 − 2 = ____   4. 4 − 3 = ____

5. 3 − 2 = ____   6. 5 − 3 = ____

ADDITION

3 + 4 = __7__

2 + 0 = __2__

Add.

1. 0 + 5 = ____
2. 3 + 2 = ____
3. 7 + 1 = ____

4. 4 + 3 = ____
5. 5 + 3 = ____
6. 5 + 2 = ____

7. 1 + 6 = ____
8. 8 + 0 = ____
9. 3 + 5 = ____

10. 4 + 1 = ____
11. 2 + 2 = ____
12. 1 + 3 = ____

SUBTRACTION

5 − 3 = __2__   3 − 0 = __3__

Subtract.

1. 4 − 3 = ____   2. 8 − 4 = ____   3. 6 − 4 = ____

4. 6 − 5 = ____   5. 5 − 1 = ____   6. 8 − 6 = ____

7. 7 − 0 = ____   8. 3 − 2 = ____   9. 7 − 5 = ____

10. 6 − 6 = ____   11. 7 − 1 = ____   12. 6 − 2 = ____

ADDITION AND SUBTRACTION

The answer to an addition problem is called the **sum**.
The answer to a subtraction problem is called the **difference**.

Add to find the sum.

1. 4 + 3
2. 2 + 6
3. 1 + 7
4. 2 + 4

5. 5 + 2
6. 5 + 3
7. 6 + 1
8. 3 + 3

Subtract to find the difference.

9. 6 − 5
10. 8 − 8
11. 8 − 2
12. 4 − 2

13. 6 − 3
14. 8 − 6
15. 7 − 5
16. 7 − 4

COUNTING ON

Counting on helps you find the sum.
To count on, start with the greater number.
Count 3 more numbers than 5. The sum is 8.

$$\begin{array}{r} 5 \\ +\ 3 \\ \hline 8 \end{array}$$ 6, 7, 8

0 1 2 3 4 5 6 7 8 9 10 11 12

Count on to find the sum.

1. 4 + 8 = ___
2. 7 + 4 = ___
3. 6 + 6 = ___

4. 5 + 5 = ___
5. 11 + 1 = ___
6. 9 + 3 = ___

7. $\begin{array}{r} 5 \\ +\ 4 \\ \hline \end{array}$
8. $\begin{array}{r} 10 \\ +\ 2 \\ \hline \end{array}$
9. $\begin{array}{r} 3 \\ +\ 7 \\ \hline \end{array}$
10. $\begin{array}{r} 8 \\ +\ 1 \\ \hline \end{array}$

11. $\begin{array}{r} 4 \\ +\ 6 \\ \hline \end{array}$
12. $\begin{array}{r} 5 \\ +\ 6 \\ \hline \end{array}$
13. $\begin{array}{r} 9 \\ +\ 2 \\ \hline \end{array}$
14. $\begin{array}{r} 7 \\ +\ 5 \\ \hline \end{array}$

COUNTING BACK

Counting back helps you find the difference.
To count back, start with the greater number.
Count 5 numbers back from 11. The difference is 6.

$$11 - 5 = 6$$ (10, 9, 8, 7, 6)

0 1 2 3 4 5 6 7 8 9 10 11 12

Count back to find the difference.

1. 11 − 4 = ___
2. 12 − 5 = ___
3. 11 − 2 = ___

4. 12 − 7 = ___
5. 9 − 3 = ___
6. 10 − 6 = ___

7. 12 − 4
8. 11 − 6
9. 11 − 7
10. 12 − 8

11. 10 − 2
12. 11 − 5
13. 12 − 6
14. 12 − 3

ADDITION USING A NUMBER LINE

A number line can help you find a sum.
Count 2 more than 5.

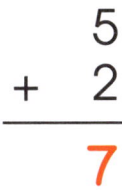
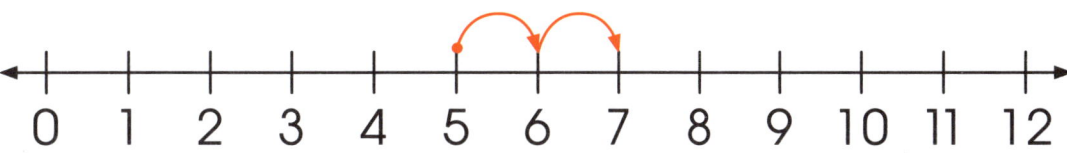

Use the number line to find the sum.

1. 7 + 2
2. 5 + 5
3. 4 + 4
4. 7 + 4

5. 8 + 4
6. 9 + 2
7. 4 + 3
8. 6 + 2

9. 7 + 5
10. 6 + 3
11. 8 + 2
12. 9 + 3

13. 5 + 3
14. 4 + 5
15. 6 + 4
16. 3 + 8

SUBTRACTION USING A NUMBER LINE

A number line can help you find a difference.
Count 3 less than 8.

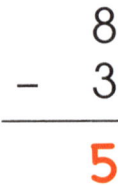
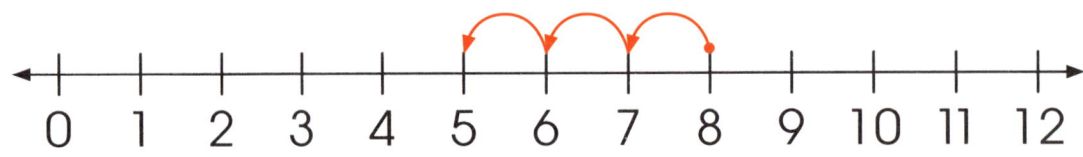

Use the number line to find the difference.

1. 11
  − 4

2. 12
  − 7

3. 8
  − 3

4. 9
  − 5

5. 7
  − 4

6. 9
  − 4

7. 10
  − 2

8. 8
  − 5

9. 9
  − 6

10. 6
  − 5

11. 12
  − 5

12. 10
  − 4

13. 12
  − 8

14. 11
  − 2

15. 9
  − 8

16. 11
  − 6

ADDITION AND SUBTRACTION

Add or subtract to find the sum or difference.

1. 8 − 3
2. 11 − 3
3. 9 + 2
4. 10 − 4

5. 6 + 3
6. 12 − 3
7. 6 + 4
8. 7 + 5

9. 11 − 5
10. 9 − 6
11. 5 + 5
12. 12 − 7

13. 8 + 2
14. 10 − 5
15. 9 + 3
16. 12 − 5

ADDITION AND SUBTRACTION

Write + or − to make the number sentences true.
The first one is done for you.

1. 9 [−] 5 = 4
2. 10 ☐ 4 = 6
3. 6 ☐ 6 = 12

4. 6 ☐ 2 = 4
5. 8 ☐ 4 = 12
6. 7 ☐ 4 = 3

7. 6 ☐ 4 = 2
8. 5 ☐ 5 = 10
9. 4 ☐ 6 = 10

10. 12 ☐ 5 = 7
11. 8 ☐ 2 = 10
12. 11 ☐ 9 = 2

13. 5 ☐ 6 = 11
14. 8 ☐ 5 = 3
15. 6 ☐ 3 = 9

PLANE FIGURES

Draw lines from the objects to the matching figures. The first one is done for you.

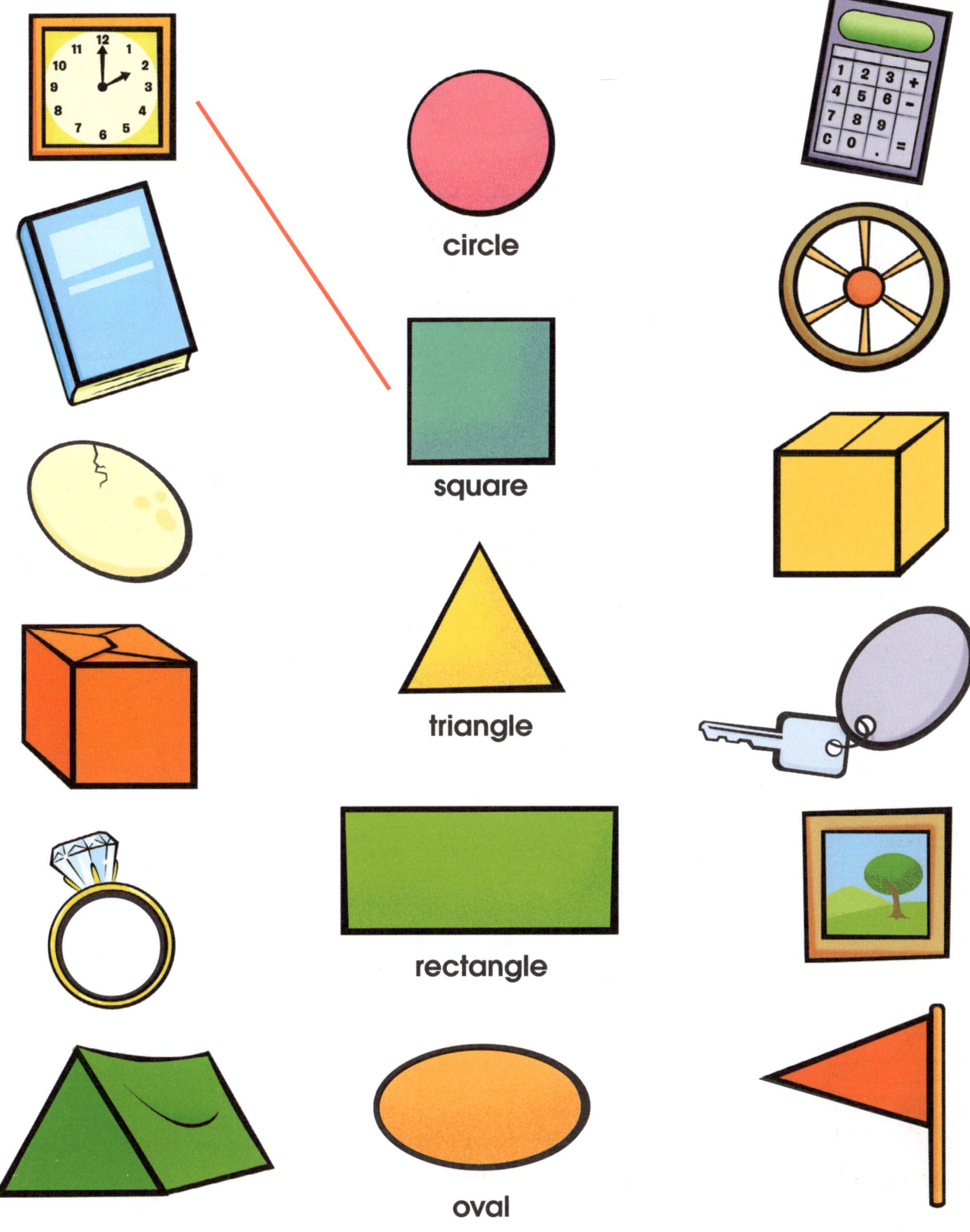

SPACE FIGURES

Draw lines from the objects to the matching figures. The first one is done for you.

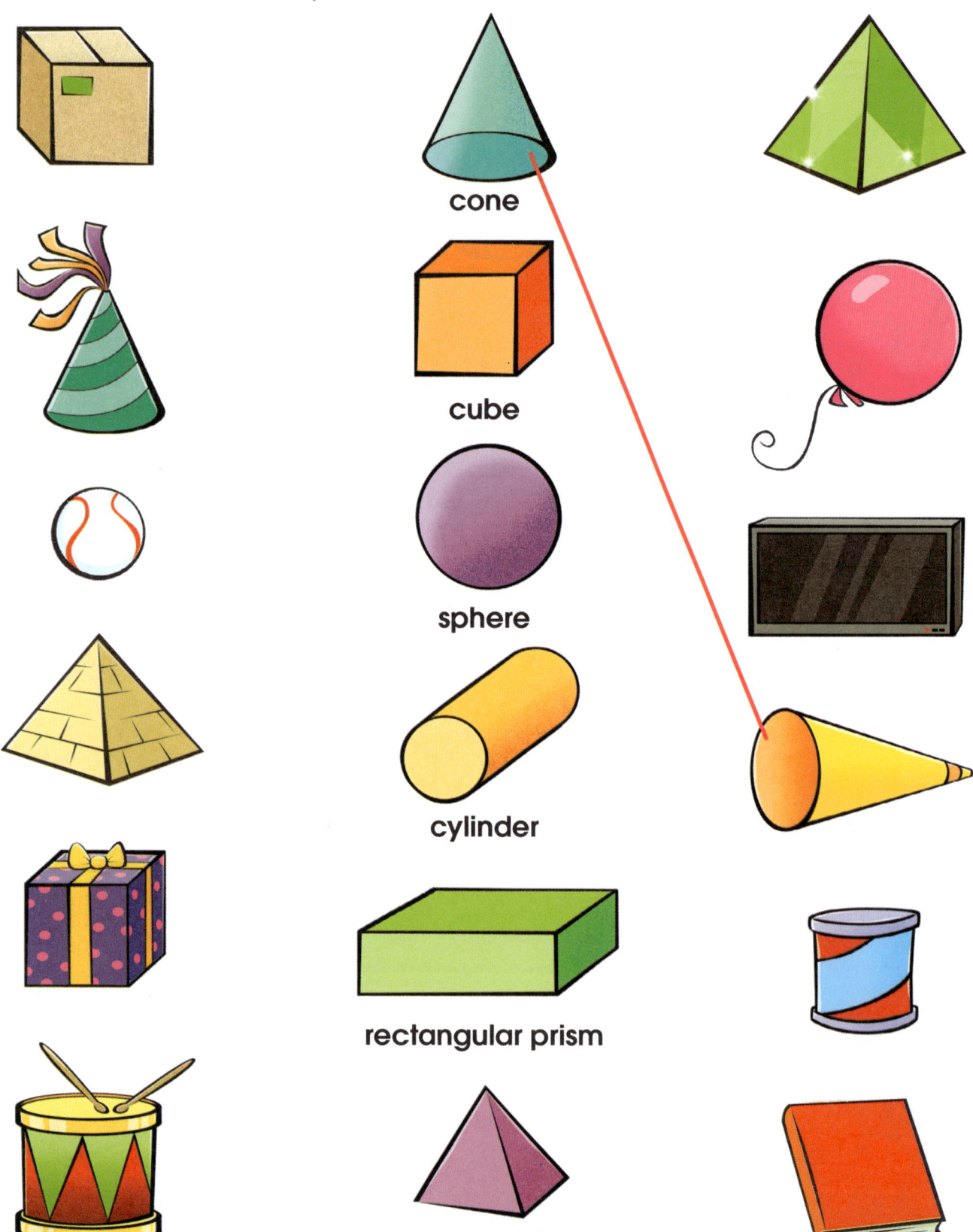

SAME SIZE AND SHAPE

Circle the shape that fits the outline.

1.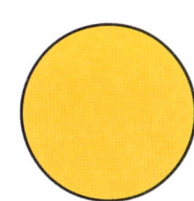

2.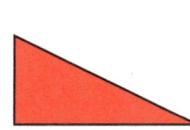

3.

4.

5.

COUNTING BY TENS

How many are there? Write the number of tens and ones.
The first one is done for you.

1.  <u> 1 </u> ten <u> 10 </u>
ten

2.  ____ tens ____
twenty

3.  ____ tens ____
thirty

4.  ____ tens ____
forty

5. 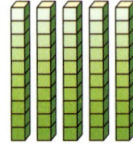 ____ tens ____
fifty

6.  ____ tens ____
sixty

7.  ____ tens ____
seventy

8.  ____ tens ____
eighty

9. 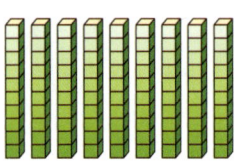 ____ tens ____
ninety

Write the missing numbers.

10. 10 20 ____ 40 50 ____ 70 80 90 100

11. 10 ____ ____ 40 ____ 60 70 ____ 90 ____

TENS AND ONES

ten __1__ ones __2__   How many s? __12__

Circle groups of ten. Write the number of tens and ones.
Then write how many there are in all.

1. ten _____ ones _____

   How many 🎾s? _____

2. tens _____ ones _____

   How many 🏐s? _____

3. tens _____ ones _____

   How many ⚽s? _____

4. tens _____ ones _____

   How many 🔴s? _____

5. ten _____ ones _____

   How many 🏐s? _____

6. ten _____ ones _____

   How many 🎾s? _____

TENS AND ONES

Read the numbers.
Write how many tens and how many ones there are.
The first one is done for you.

		tens	ones			tens	ones
1.	65	6	5	2.	28	___	___

		tens	ones			tens	ones
3.	54	___	___	4.	66	___	___

		tens	ones			tens	ones
5.	40	___	___	6.	34	___	___

		tens	one			ten	ones
7.	81	___	___	8.	17	___	___

		tens	ones			tens	one
9.	30	___	___	10.	71	___	___

		ten	ones			tens	ones
11.	19	___	___	12.	25	___	___

GREATER THAN AND LESS THAN

Greater means more than.
Less means not as many.

Circle the number that is greater.
The first one is done for you.

1. 13   (31)
2. 35   27
3. 50   48
4. 43   34
5. 10   15
6. 25   31
7. 18   10
8. 21   19
9. 23   14

Circle the number that is less.
The first one is done for you.

10. (44)   54
11. 18   13
12. 81   18
13. 78   82
14. 25   31
15. 23   36
16. 20   30
17. 62   59
18. 55   48

BEFORE, BETWEEN AND AFTER

Write the number that comes **before**.

1. ___ 45
2. ___ 27
3. ___ 24
4. ___ 33

5. ___ 81
6. ___ 30
7. ___ 18
8. ___ 67

Write the number that comes **between**.

9. 91 ___ 93
10. 53 ___ 55
11. 40 ___ 42

12. 24 ___ 26
13. 17 ___ 19
14. 36 ___ 38

Write the number that comes **after**.

15. 6 ___
16. 47 ___
17. 25 ___
18. 19 ___

19. 92 ___
20. 50 ___
21. 74 ___
22. 11 ___

COUNTING COINS

front   back   5c   10c   15c   20c

5 cents = 5c

To count five-cent coins, count by fives.

front   back   10c   20c   30c   40c

10 cents = 10c

To count ten-cent coins, count by tens.

front   back   20c   40c   60c   80c

20 cents = 20c

To count twenty-cent coins, count by twenties.

Count the coins. Write each amount.

1.       _____c

2.       _____c

3.     _____c

COUNTING COINS

How much do the clothes cost?
Count on to find the total amounts.
Write the totals on the price tags.

1.

___ ___ ___ ___ ___ ___

2.

___ ___ ___ ___ ___ ___ ___

3.

___ ___ ___ ___ ___ ___ ___

4.

___ ___ ___ ___ ___ ___

5.

___ ___ ___ ___ ___

Counting Coins

TIME: HOURS

A clock has two hands.
The short hand shows the **hours**.
The long hand shows the **minutes**.

minute hand

hour hand

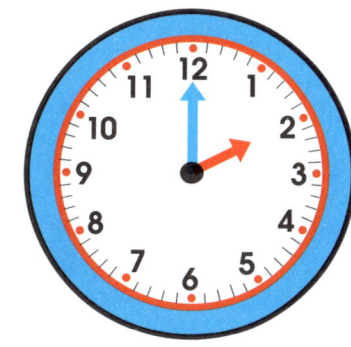

__2__ o'clock

__2__ : __00__

When the long hand points to the 12, we say o'clock.
To which hour does the short hand point?

Write the time.

 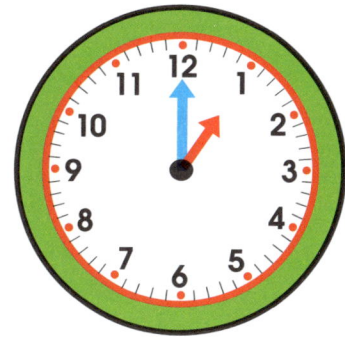 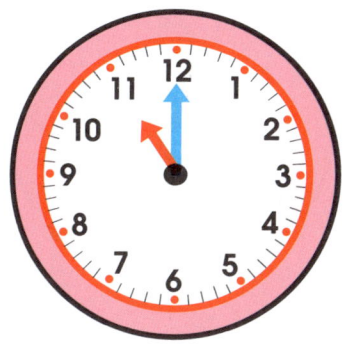

1. _____ o'clock   2. _____ o'clock   3. _____ o'clock

   ____ : ____   ____ : ____   ____ : ____

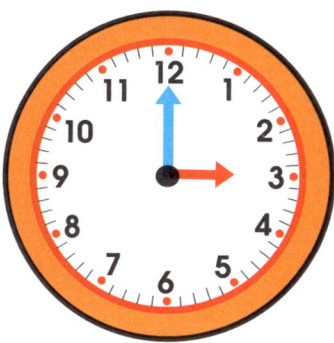  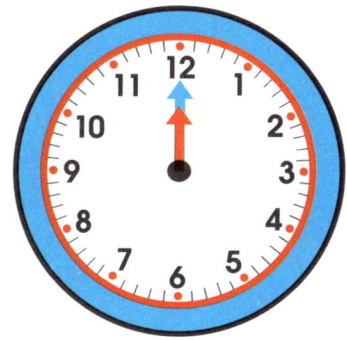

4. _____ o'clock   5. _____ o'clock   6. _____ o'clock

   ____ : ____   ____ : ____   ____ : ____

TIME: HALF HOURS

When the minute hand points to the 6, it is half past the hour. The hour hand is halfway between the current and next hour.

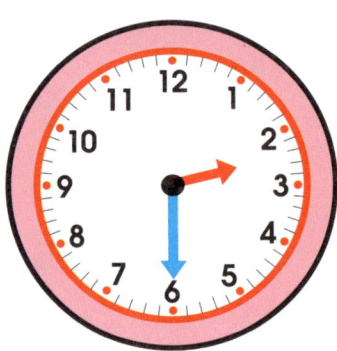

Half past __2__

__2__ : __30__

Write the time.

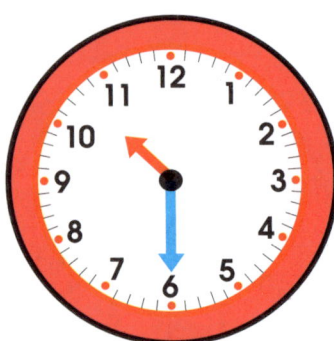

1. Half past _____

   _____ : _____

2. Half past _____

   _____ : _____

3. Half past _____

   _____ : _____

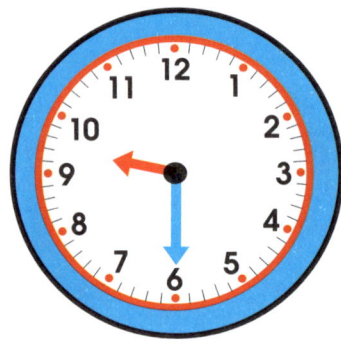

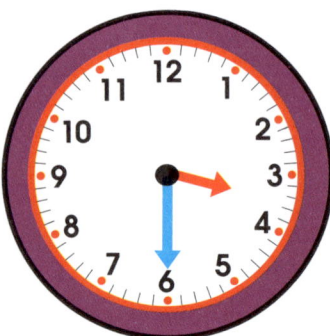

4. Half past _____

   _____ : _____

5. Half past _____

   _____ : _____

6. Half past _____

   _____ : _____

TIME: QUARTER PAST THE HOUR

When the minute hand points to the 3, it is a quarter past the hour. The hour hand is a little past the hour.

Quarter past __2__

__2__ : __15__

Write the time.

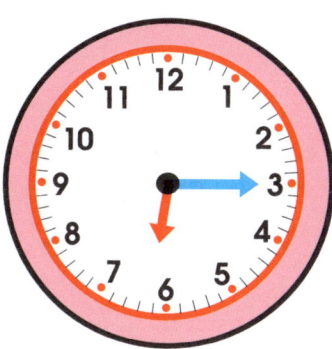

1. Quarter past _____
   _____ : _____

2. Quarter past _____
   _____ : _____

3. Quarter past _____
   _____ : _____

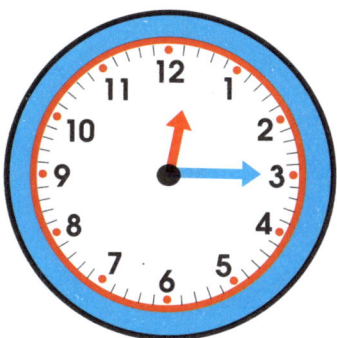

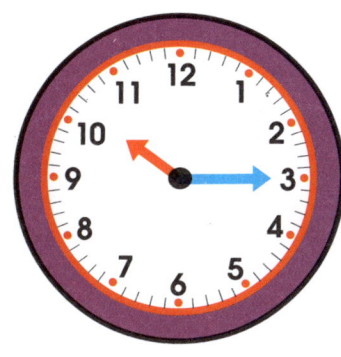

4. Quarter past _____
   _____ : _____

5. Quarter past _____
   _____ : _____

6. Quarter past _____
   _____ : _____

TIME: QUARTER TO THE HOUR

When the minute hand points to the 9, it is a quarter to the next hour. The hour hand is closer to the next hour.

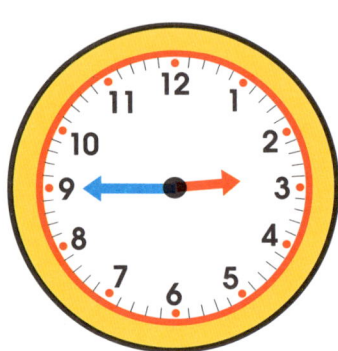

Quarter to __3__

__2__ : __45__

Write the time.

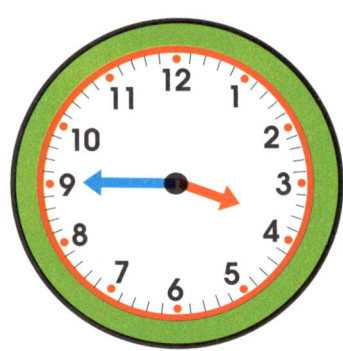

1. Quarter to _____

   _____ : _____

2. Quarter to _____

   _____ : _____

3. Quarter to _____

   _____ : _____

4. Quarter to _____

   _____ : _____

5. Quarter to _____

   _____ : _____

6. Quarter to _____

   _____ : _____

EQUAL PARTS OF WHOLES

This shape has two equal parts.
Each part is $\frac{1}{2}$ or one-half of the whole.

Find the shapes that show one-half.
Write $\frac{1}{2}$ in each part.

1.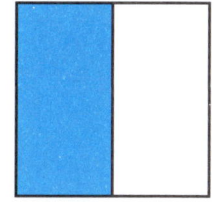
2.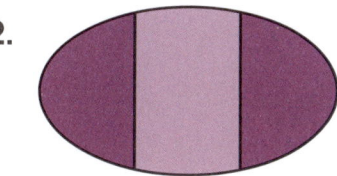
3.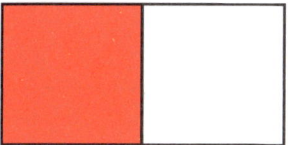

4.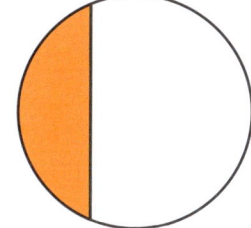
5.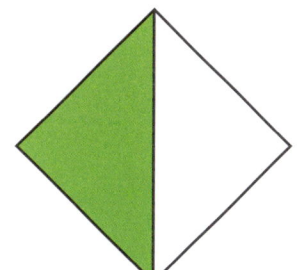
6.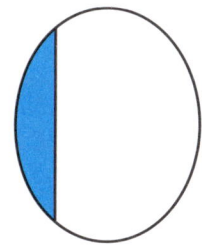

Colour $\frac{1}{2}$ of each shape.

7.
8.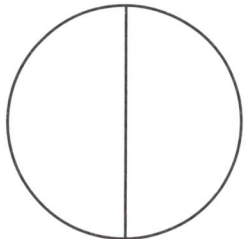
9.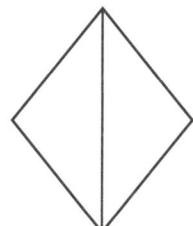

10.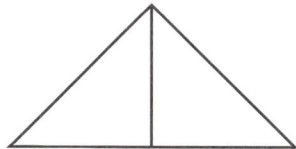
11.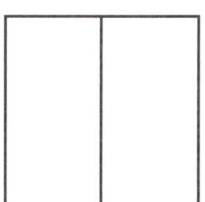
12.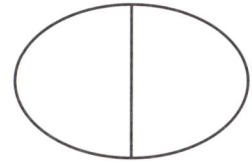

HALVES, THIRDS AND QUARTERS

A **fraction** names a part of a whole.
The bottom of a fraction tells how many parts there are in all.

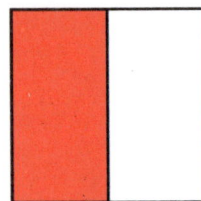   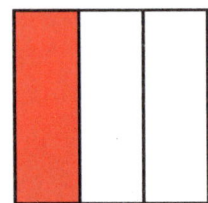   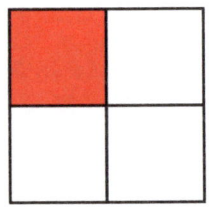

1 of 2 equal parts is $\frac{1}{2}$.   1 of 3 equal parts is $\frac{1}{3}$.   1 of 4 equal parts is $\frac{1}{4}$.

Count the parts of each shape. Write the number in the box to make a fraction. The first one is done for you.

1. 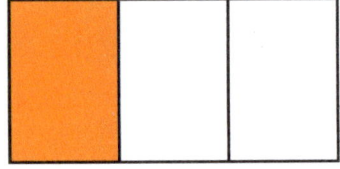 $\frac{1}{3}$

2. 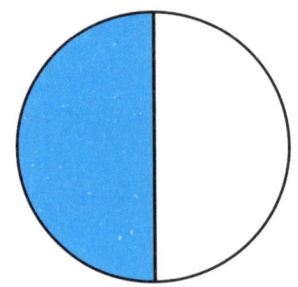 $\frac{1}{\Box}$

3. 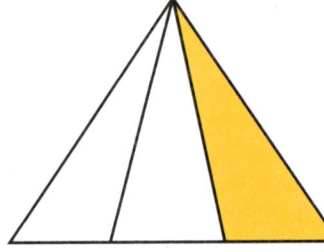 $\frac{1}{\Box}$

4. 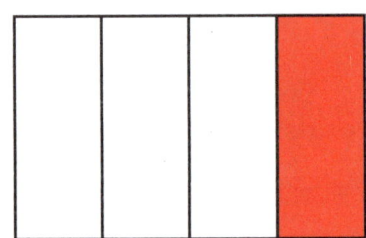 $\frac{1}{\Box}$

5. 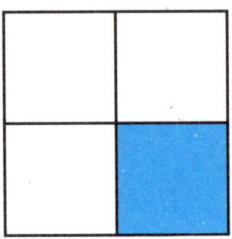 $\frac{1}{\Box}$

6. 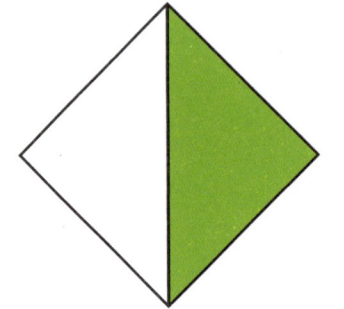 $\frac{1}{\Box}$

PARTS OF GROUPS

A **fraction** can also name a part of a group.

1 of 3 equal parts is $\frac{1}{3}$.

Circle the objects to show each fraction.

1. $\frac{1}{4}$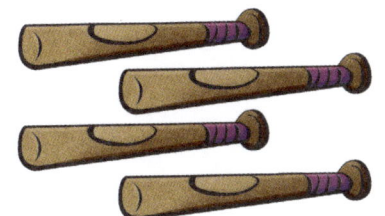

2. $\frac{1}{2}$

3. $\frac{1}{3}$

4. $\frac{1}{2}$

5. $\frac{1}{4}$

6. $\frac{1}{3}$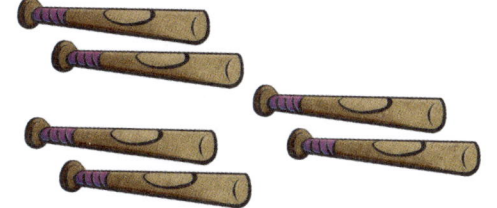

7. $\frac{1}{2}$

8. $\frac{1}{4}$

PICTURE GRAPH

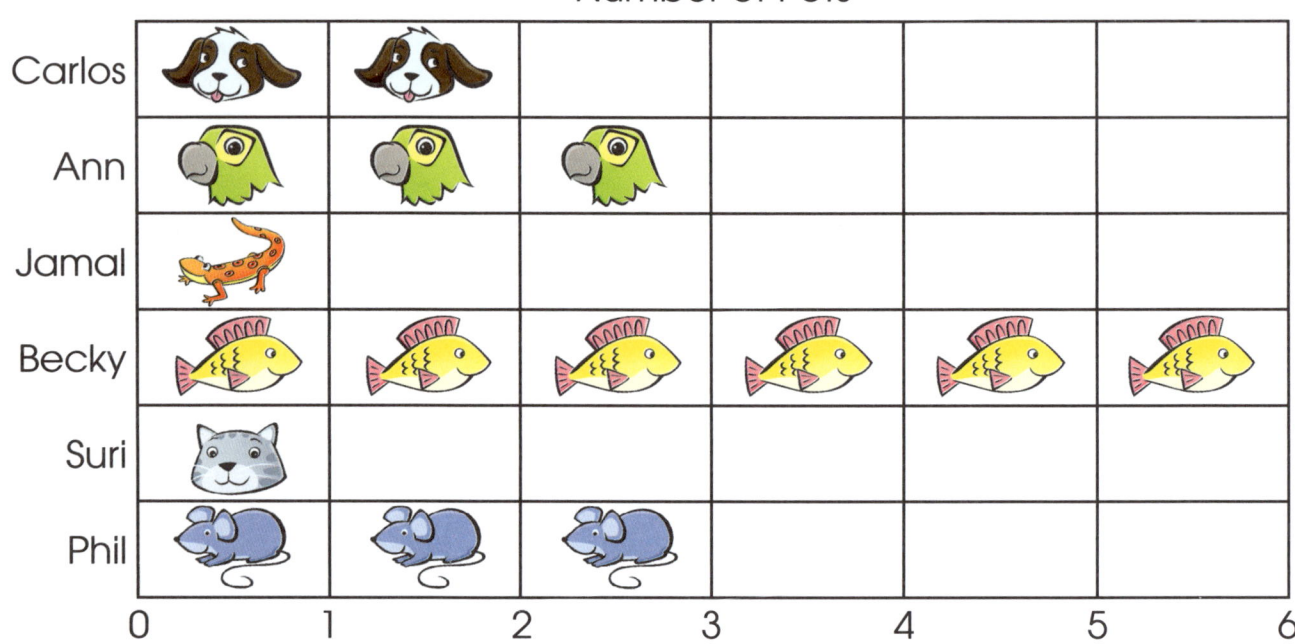

Use the picture graph to answer the questions.
How many pets does each child have?

1. Carlos _____
2. Becky _____
3. Ann _____

4. Suri _____
5. Jamal _____
6. Phil _____

7. How many pets do Carlos and Phil have in all?

8. Becky has more pets than Ann.
How many more pets does Becky have?

ADDING THREE ADDENDS

An **addend** is a number in an addition problem. Follow these steps to add three addends:

1. Add two of the numbers. Look for a double or numbers with a sum of 10 to make it easier. $3 + 3 = 6$
2. Add the sum to the third number. $6 + 4 = 10$
3. Write the sum. $3 + 3 + 4 = 10$

$$\begin{array}{r} 3 \\ 3 \\ + 4 \\ \hline 10 \end{array}$$

Add.

1. 3
    2
  + 5
  ___

2. 1
    2
  + 8
  ___

3. 3
    1
  + 7
  ___

4. 5
    5
  + 2
  ___

5. 6
    2
  + 2
  ___

6. 4
    4
  + 4
  ___

7. 2
    6
  + 3
  ___

8. 2
    4
  + 5
  ___

9. 4
    7
  + 1
  ___

10. 1
    8
  + 3
  ___

11. 4
    4
  + 2
  ___

12. 9
    1
  + 2
  ___

ADDING TENS AND ONES

Follow these steps to add tens and ones:

1. Add the ones.
2. Add the tens.

Step 1
tens ones
24
+ 13
―――
 7

Step 2
tens ones
24
+ 13
―――
37

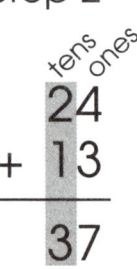

Add to find the sum.

1. 27
   + 60
   ―――

2. 25
   + 3
   ―――

3. 91
   + 6
   ―――

4. 45
   + 14
   ―――

5. 44
   + 34
   ―――

6. 52
   + 6
   ―――

7. 60
   + 8
   ―――

8. 83
   + 6
   ―――

9. 72
   + 1
   ―――

10. 63
   + 5
   ―――

11. 13
   + 4
   ―――

12. 25
   + 22
   ―――

SUBTRACTING TENS AND ONES

Follow these steps to subtract tens and ones:

1. Subtract the ones.
2. Subtract the tens.

Step 1
```
 tens ones
  5  7
-  1  2
  ―――――
        5
```

Step 2
```
 tens ones
  5  7
-  1  2
  ―――――
  4  5
```

Subtract to find the difference.

1. 38
   − 6
   ―――

2. 24
   − 3
   ―――

3. 57
   − 5
   ―――

4. 98
   − 6
   ―――

5. 25
   − 2
   ―――

6. 49
   − 7
   ―――

7. 47
   − 15
   ―――

8. 65
   − 22
   ―――

9. 86
   − 26
   ―――

10. 96
    − 23
    ―――

11. 78
    − 54
    ―――

12. 48
    − 34
    ―――

RACE TO THE MONKEYS

Take turns giving the answer to every other problem. The player who has the most correct answers wins.

3 tens + 7 ones = _____

Start

3 + 4

6 − 3

8 + 2

17 − 15

9 + 3

36 − 24

13 + 6 = _____

16 + 10

12 − 7

11 + 25

19 − ☐ = 16

8 + 4

12 − 3

19 − 12

☐ + 6 = 12

18 + 11

12 − ☐ = 8

10 − 3

6 tens + 4 ones = _____

10 + 8

15 − ☐ = 10

22 − 11

23 − ☐ = 10

11 − 7

20 + 10

18 + 11

11 − ☐ = 7

6 + ☐ = 14

10 + ☐ = 12

32 − ☐ = 20

Finish

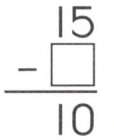

ANSWER KEY

Page 2
1. dog
2. cat
3. fish
4. bird

Page 3
1. fan, lamp
2. apple, bat
3. ant, ham
4. map, cat

Page 4
1. egg, tent
2. web, bed
3. net, jet
4. ten, nest

Page 5
1. bib, wig
2. ship, six
3. fish, mittens
4. pig, pin

Page 6
1. fox, clock
2. doll, lock
3. box, rocket
4. socks, mop

Page 7
1. sun, rug
2. cup, bus
3. gum, cupcake
4. duck, tub

Page 8

Page 9
1. ten 2. cat 3. pig
4. bus 5. doll 6. fan
7. fish 8. nest 9. duck

Page 10
1. snail
2. cake
3. rain
4. day
5. grate, gate

Page 11
1. three
2. tree
3. sheep
4. leaf
5. he, me

Page 12
1. bike
2. nine
3. ice
4. right
5. tight, tie

Page 13
1. goat
2. rope
3. boat
4. rose
5. nose, note

Page 14
1. tube
2. glue
3. huge
4. cute
5. few, new

Page 15

(crossword: rake, bike, tube, bee, kite, one, slide)

Page 16

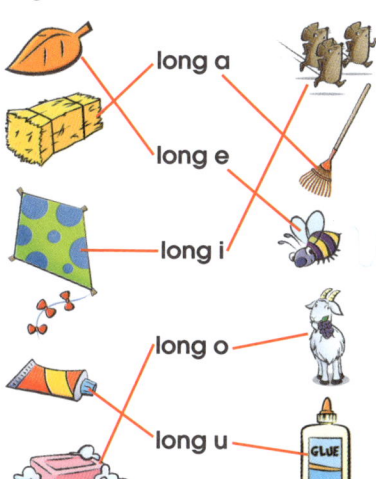

Page 17

4 1 3
5 6 2

Page 18
1. <u>our</u> dog is hungry.
2. <u>dad</u> brings food.
3. <u>skip</u> eats quickly.
4. <u>food</u> goes on the floor.
5. <u>dogs</u> are messy.
6. <u>now</u> I need to clean up.
7. Answers will vary.

Page 19
1. <u>is</u> Mother home?
2. <u>where</u> did she go?
3. <u>when</u> will she be back?
4. <u>who</u> baked the cookies?
5. <u>they</u> are good.
6. <u>may</u> I have another one?
7. Answers will vary.

Page 20
1. Dad
2. farmer
3. cow
4. dog
5. chicken

Page 21
Places / Things
zoo / book
house / pizza
town / bike
Answers will vary. Make sure words name a place or a thing.

Page 22
1. dogs
2. spots
3. ears
4. cats
5. bones

Page 23
1. play
2. hits
3. flies
4. runs
5. catch

Page 24
1. plants
2. grows
3. pulls
4. waters
5. eats

Page 25
1. hot
2. loud
3. cold
4. soft
5. wet

Page 26
1. big
2. three
3. striped
4. black
5. little
6. four
7. Answers will vary. Make sure describing word is underlined.

Page 27
1. don't
2. aren't
3. haven't
4. Let's
5. won't

Page 28
1. 4   2. 2
3. 4   4. 4
5. 5   6. 3

Page 29
1. 2   2. 2
3. 3   4. 1
5. 1   6. 2

Page 30
1. 5   2. 5   3. 8
4. 7   5. 8   6. 7
7. 7   8. 8   9. 8
10. 5 11. 4 12. 4

ANSWER KEY

Page 31
1. 1   2. 4   3. 2
4. 1   5. 4   6. 2
7. 7   8. 1   9. 2
10. 0 11. 6 12. 4

Page 32
1. 7   2. 8   3. 8   4. 6
5. 7   6. 8   7. 7   8. 6
9. 1   10. 0 11. 6 12. 2
13. 3 14. 2 15. 2 16. 3

Page 33
1. 12   2. 11   3. 12
4. 10   5. 12   6. 12
7. 9   8. 12   9. 10   10. 9
11. 10 12. 11 13. 11 14. 12

Page 34
1. 7   2. 7   3. 9
4. 5   5. 6   6. 4
7. 8   8. 5   9. 4   10. 4
11. 8 12. 6 13. 6 14. 9

Page 35
1. 9   2. 10   3. 8   4. 11
5. 12   6. 11   7. 7   8. 8
9. 12   10. 9   11. 10 12. 12
13. 8   14. 9   15. 10 16. 11

Page 36
1. 7   2. 5   3. 5   4. 4
5. 3   6. 5   7. 8   8. 3
9. 3   10. 1 11. 7 12. 6
13. 4 14. 9 15. 1 16. 5

Page 37
1. 5   2. 8   3. 11   4. 6
5. 9   6. 9   7. 10   8. 12
9. 6   10. 3 11. 10 12. 5
13. 10 14. 5 15. 12 16. 7

Page 38
1. −   2. −   3. +
4. −   5. +   6. −
7. −   8. +   9. +
10. − 11. + 12. −
13. + 14. − 15. +

Page 39

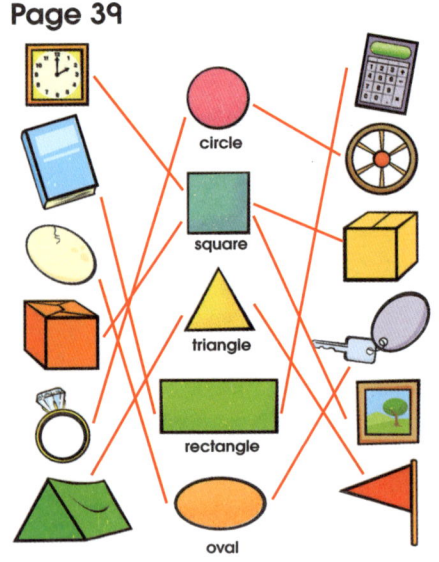

Page 40

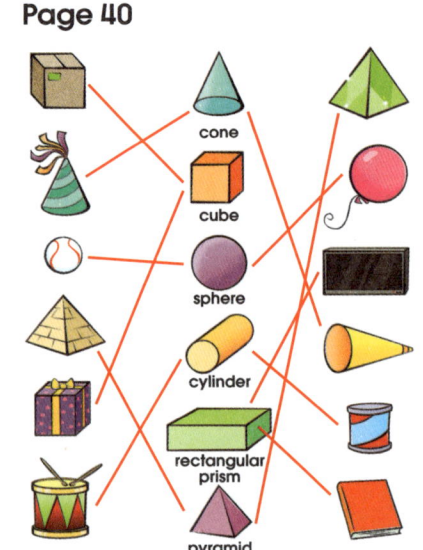

Page 41

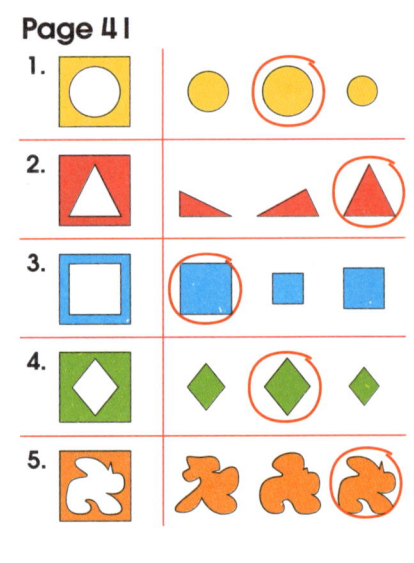

Page 42
1. 1 ten 10   2. 2 tens 20
3. 3 tens 30   4. 4 tens 40
5. 5 tens 50   6. 6 tens 60
7. 7 tens 70   8. 8 tens 80
9. 9 tens 90
10. 10, 20, **30**, 40, 50, **60**, 70, 80, 90, 100
11. 10, **20**, **30**, 40, **50**, 60, 70, **80**, 90, **100**

Page 43
1. ten 1   ones 5   2. tens 2   ones 2
   15   22
3. tens 3 ones 4   4. tens 2   ones 0
   34   20
5. ten 1   ones 7   6. ten 1   ones 8
   17   18

Page 44
	tens	ones		tens	ones
1.	6	5	2.	2	8
3.	5	4	4.	6	6
5.	4	0	6.	3	4
7.	8	1	8.	1	7
9.	3	0	10.	7	1
11.	1	9	12.	2	5

Page 45
1. 31   2. 35   3. 50
4. 43   5. 15   6. 31
7. 18   8. 21   9. 23
10. 44 11. 13 12. 18
13. 78 14. 25 15. 23
16. 20 17. 59 18. 48

Page 46
1. 44   2. 26   3. 23   4. 32
5. 80   6. 29   7. 17   8. 66
9. 92   10. 54 11. 41
12. 25 13. 18 14. 37
15. 7   16. 48 17. 26 18. 20
19. 93 20. 51 21. 75 22. 12

ANSWER KEY

Page 47
1. 30c
2. 60c
3. 80c

Page 48
1. 20c, 40c, 50c, 60c, 65c, 70c; 70c
2. 20c, 30c, 40c, 45c, 50c, 55c, 60c; 60c
3. 20c, 40c, 60c, 70c, 80c, 90c, 95c; 95c
4. 20c, 40c, 50c, 55c, 60c, 65c; 65c
5. 20c, 40c, 60c, 80c, 90c, 95c; 95c

Page 49
1. 7 o'clock 7:00
2. 1 o'clock 1:00
3. 11 o'clock 11:00
4. 3 o'clock 3:00
5. 5 o'clock 5:00
6. 12 o'clock 12:00

Page 50
1. Half past 10 10:30
2. Half past 4 4:30
3. Half past 9 9:30
4. Half past 3 3:30
5. Half past 8 8:30
6. Half past 6 6:30

Page 51
1. Quarter past 6 6:15
2. Quarter past 8 8:15
3. Quarter past 1 1:15
4. Quarter past 12 12:15
5. Quarter past 10 10:15
6. Quarter past 7 7:15

Page 52
1. Quarter to 4 3:45
2. Quarter to 9 8:45
3. Quarter to 1 12:45
4. Quarter to 7 6:45
5. Quarter to 2 1:45
6. Quarter to 10 9:45

Page 53
(Section coloured can vary.)

Page 54
1. 1/3
2. 1/2
3. 1/3
4. 1/4
5. 1/4
6. 1/2

Page 55
1. 1/4
2. 1/2
3. 1/3
4. 1/2
5. 1/4
6. 1/3
7. 1/2
8. 1/4

Objects circled can vary.

Page 56
1. 2   2. 6   3. 3
4. 1   5. 1   6. 3
7. 2 + 3 = 5
8. 6 − 3 = 3

Page 57
1. 10   2. 11   3. 11   4. 12
5. 10   6. 12   7. 11   8. 11
9. 12   10. 12   11. 10   12. 12

Page 58
1. 87   2. 28   3. 97   4. 59
5. 78   6. 58   7. 68   8. 89
9. 73   10. 68   11. 17   12. 47

Page 59
1. 32   2. 21   3. 52   4. 92
5. 23   6. 42   7. 32   8. 43
9. 60   10. 73   11. 24   12. 14

Page 60

Start				3 tens + 7 ones = 37
+3/4 = 7				10+8=18 / 18+11=29
6−3=3	16+10=26	12−7=5	11+25=36	15−5=10 / 11−4=7
8+2=10	19−3=16		18+11=29	22−11=11 / 6+8=14
17−15=2	8+4=12		12−4=8	23−13=10 / 10+2=12
9+3=12	12−3=9		10−3=7	11−7=4 / 32−12=20
36−24=12	19−12=7			20+10=30 / Finish
13+6=19	6+6=12	6 tens + 4 ones = 64